# To Be or Not to Be Religious

### Paradox of a progressive world

(Revised Edition April 2024)

*Prof. Dr. Christopher Thomas Ph.D.*

NOTION PRESS

NOTION PRESS

India. Singapore. Malaysia.

ISBN 979 889363135 7

# Dedication

*This Book is dedicated to*
*All peace-loving, inquisitive, harmonious individuals*
*Without concern of their religious divide*
*For a Better Tolerant World*

# About the Author

The author Prof. Dr. Christopher Thomas is a naturalist who believes that this world, our dear earth is very significant but just a minute spec of the vast universe and whatever occurred in this world have occurred through evolution through ages including its formation and reached a stage we presently live in. Modern science has explained us all this to a great extent. Whether there is a Super Power controlling its inhabitants from anywhere above or below other than nature itself is a matter of perspectives and debate, he contemplates.

An academician, Dr. Thomas has acquired vast world knowhow from his eighty plus years of life expertise, educations in various subjects and fields, and has already published several heavy and light reading books in Philosophy, Psychology, Sociology, as well as on religious topics.

According to his views and opinion, humans are still evolving to a higher level of more sophisticated more intelligent human species among all other organisms and it is not yet time for us to decide whether the world is in its last leg of improvement or otherwise as some unscrupulous discourteous groups propagate. With regard to religions, faith, spirituality and worships, they will still go on perhaps in heterogeneous forms and kinds until humans survive because religiosity provide humans as a harbor of refuge at times of their predicaments and with sense of peace when their minds are distressed and no earthly elucidations at site.

We have immense pleasure in introducing this exceptionally informative utilitarian volume produced from miscellaneous researches through accessible historical, archeological, as well scientific data and with a modern outlook envisioned for the present society to learn from and to form their own opinions based on ideologies of this book. We hope it will influence our cherished readers' minds to have better stance on the subjects expressed and so take pride in presenting this volume to our esteemed readers.

To contact the author and for more information about his other books namely:

Learning About Life (English) ISBN81-76662-298-2;

Jeevitha Vijayathinte Padavukal (Malayalam) ISBN978-81-8449-354-2;

Life A Tribute (English) ISBN14515889127;

Winning Wisdom (English) ISBN1453745998 & 9781636332666;

An Ideal society (English) ISBN1453733353 & 9781636693620;

Our Human Rights (English) ISBN9781470018016;

A Shortcut Through The Bible (English) ISBN978-93-80151-46-5 & 1453747907;

The Incredible Universe (English) 978-93-80151-70-0; & 1456410989

Sajeeva Loka Mathangal (Malayalam) ISBN978-81-8465-482-0;

*Visit www.ChristopherThomas.in. /*
*www.amazon.com*

**Publishers**

# Preface

Prof. Dr. Christopher Thomas reiterates that Religion and God are concepts originated and being followed by many in the world from prehistoric days as proven by archeological findings as well as from available written history of humans from around 6000 years behind us. If the ape-man or cave-man imagined and feared a supernatural power above him and called it/him God out of fear of things beyond his percepts such as natural catastrophes etc. you name them, and began to worship that god/spirit to satisfy it and escape from its wrath; modern man today in this era of information and knowledge also worshipping God for the same reason is a matter of ignominy. Some people claim that *God* is a myth and religion just mythology, nothing else. It is true that this subject is a matter of continued debate and that is the reason why it exists today in some manner or other. As a matter of fact, holding humanity in fear under their thumps and to benefit from such suppression and misleads in numerous forms is advantageous to some or many people and can be considered a ransom deed.

It is true that human as a whole is still in the process of evolution and he is subjected to various conditions beyond his own capabilities to reckon with for which he has no control too and hence tends to believe and carried away by the merchants of religion. Eventually when he attains intellect at its best and recognize his own potentials there will probably be no need for him to believe in any external powers other than his own brains and its capabilities to manage life. We all know that there are some imprudent people who adore the mask of religion and do every shameful misdeed to lead a fabulous life.

Our world itself is just a spec in the universe, we are here in the present forms after series of evolution, and we are still in the slow process of evolving towards better creations. There is no need for us to worry about our existence as long as we realize that evolution will not drastically end anytime soon nor the world itself vanish like some spiritual chaperons shout from the hill tops and podiums. For now, our mission in the world is to empower our generation with scientific and technological knowledge available to us and let them decide if God is alone responsible for our future if we forsake our part to do our callings. Humanity is striving towards this goal.

The contents of this book are not written with any specific religious teachings or practices in mind but on a general outlook. It aims to bring together certain universal knowledge in an unbiased point of view. It is also aimed at enlightening hardcore religious agents that humanity is our top priority in this world to reconcile, above both politics and religiosity.

History teaches us that several small and large religious and ethnic battles were fought in various parts of the world in the past and continues even today, but as we learn, they only gave hatred and distress to human kind, and mass destruction, nothing less. Is it not time for the new generation to look forward to the betterment of humanity beyond the horizons of religions? I think yes, and hope this book will help my readers to think seriously and should empower many to do so.

Prof. Dr. Christopher Thomas Ph.D.

# Table of Contents

# Chapter 1

# Origin of Universe and the Earth

From archeological and scientific opinion and available data till date, the conception is that our universe began with a *Big Bang* starting from extremely high density and temperature. Space expanded, the universe cooled and the simplest elements formed. Gravity gradually drew matter together to form the first stars and the first galaxies.

**Formation and evolution of the universe**

The *Big Bang* theory says that the universe came into being from a single unimaginable hot and dense point (*aka a singularity*) more than 13 billion years ago. It did not occur in an already existing space. Rather it initiated the expansion and cooling of space itself. Recent studies also say the universe is still expanding. Scientists now consider it unlikely the universe has an end. A region where the galaxies stop or where there would be a barrier of some kind should be marking the end of space. Astronomers once thought the universe could collapse in a big crunch like it began. Now most of them agree that it will end with a big freeze trillions of years in the future, long after earth is destroyed, the universe will drift apart until galaxy and star formation ceases; according to some latest studies. At this stage, they are only perceptions based on various studies. As time passes new theories may come to stay, either in same line or much different.

## Formation of Earth

Our dear earth was estimated to have formed about 4.5 billion years ago. When the solar system settled into its current layout, earth formed when gravity pulled swirling gas and dust into becoming the third planet from the sun. Like its fellow terrestrial planets, earth has a central core, a rocky mantle, and a solid crust. The earth is about one third of the age of the universe, by the creation from the solar nebula. Then hellish conditions meant earth resembled Venus for a time, with hazy, steamy atmosphere. But as the planet cooled, lava became rock and liquid water started to condense forming earth's first ocean. The oldest minerals found on earth, are called 'zircons' which date back to this period, 4.4 billion years ago.

# Chapter 2

# Beginning of Life on Earth

Studies show that life began on earth at least 3.5 to 3.8 billion years ago because, it is the age of the oldest rocks found with fossil evidence of life on earth. The earliest life forms we know of were microscopic organisms (*microbes*) that left hints of their presence in rocks.

It seems possible that the origin of life on the earth's surface could have been first prevented by an enormous flux of impacting comets and asteroids. Then a much less intense rain of comets many have deposited the very materials that allowed life to form 3.5 to 3.8 billion years ago. That means life on earth started at the end of this period called the '*late heavy bombardment.*'

*Prokaryotes* were the earliest life forms; simple creatures that fed on carbon components that were accumulating in earth's early oceans. Slowly other organisms evolved that used the sun's energy, along with compounds such as sulfides, to generate their own energy.

**Evolution of Animals**

In the animal kingdom, first groups of reptile-like animals evolved about 320 million years ago. The idea that birds evolved from reptiles appeared in 1861, only a few years after Darwin published *'On the origin of Species'*, with the discovery of an exquisite skeleton of a Late Jurassic (150 million years old) bird from Germany. The earliest reptiles evolved from a *Sauropsid* ancestor by about 320 million years ago. About 250 million years ago, transition to mammals began in the form of mammal-like reptiles. Mammals evolved from a group of reptiles called the *Synapsids*. These reptiles arose during the *Pennsylvanian period* (310-275 million years ago)

## Evolution of Birds

*Archaeopteryx* is the earliest undisputed bird. A weak flyer, it shared characteristics with its dinosaur ancestor. Those birds had teeth like dinosaur, a long bony tail, and grasping claws on its wings but also had a bird-like hip and feathers.

## Evolution of Mammals

The earliest known mammals were the *Morganucodons* (Glamorgan teeth), tiny screw-like creatures that lived in the shadows of dinosaurs some 200 million years. They were one of the different mammal lineages that emerged around that time. All living mammals today, including humans, descended from the one line that survived.

## Beginning of Vegetation

Plants first appeared about 500 million years ago, during the *Cambrian period*, when the development of multicellular animal species took off. The very first plants on land were tiny, very early as 470 million years ago. Vascular plants developed the ability to grow large and tall, and the forests developed during the *Devonian times* about 419 to 359 million years ago.

**Early Humans**

A *human* is anyone who belongs to the genius *Homo* (Latin for 'man'). Scientists still don't know exactly when or how the first humans evolved, but they have identified a few of the oldest ones. The first human ancestors are said to have appeared between five million and seven million years ago, probably when some apelike creatures in Africa began to walk habitually on two legs. Most scientists currently recognize some 15 to 20 different species of early humans. The earliest known humans are *Homo habilis* or 'handy man' who lived about 2.4 million to 1.4 million years ago in Eastern and Southern Africa.

Others include *Homo Rudolfensis,* who lived in Eastern Africa (Kenya) about 1.9 million to 1.8 million years ago, and *Homo erectus* the 'upright man' who ranged from Southern Africa all the way to modern-day China and Indonesia from about 1.89 million to 110,000 years ago.

**Modern Humans**

Modern Humans originated in Africa within the past 200,000 years and evolved from their most likely recent ancestor *Homo-Erectus* which means Upright Man in Latin.

Modern humans inhabited India around 120,000 years and 65,000 years ago according to different records. Intelligent life evolved on earth as estimated is since *Homo-Erectus* evolved, say about 1 million years ago.

# Chapter 3

# Humans and the Origin of Religions

The exact period when humans first became religious remains unknown. It was certainly a gradual process. However, researches in Evolutionary Archaeology indicate credible evidence of religious-cum-ritualistic behaviors from around the *Middle Paleolithic era* (45 to 200 thousand years ago).

**Prehistoric Evidence of Religion**

Religion has been a factor of the human experience throughout history, from pre-historic to modern times. Written history is only some 6,000 years old. Prehistorical religion history is being derived from archeological records and other indirect sources, and from suppositions. Prehistoric religion is a matter of continued debate, for this reason.

It is believed that religious behavior emerged by the *Upper Paleolithic*, between 30,000 years ago at the latest, but behavioral patterns such as burial rites reach back into the *Middle Paleolithic* coinciding with the first appearance of *Homo Neanderthals* and possibly, *Homo Naledi*.

People in the ancient world did not always believe in the gods; religious belief is a default setting for humans. The *Vedic religion* was the historical predecessor of modern Hinduism which is the first religion of modern humans. It is said, humans may have developed religion as a way to promote co-operation in social groups. Many Pagan faiths continued through practices of *Protohistoric Bronze and Iron Age* societies. Religious practices were certainly present during the *Upper Paleolithic* period dating to about 50,000 through 12,000 years ago.

In the modern history of humans, sometimes called the official religion of ancient Persia, Zoroastrianism, is the oldest surviving religion in the Middle East, with its teachings older than Buddhism, older than Judaism and far older than Christianity or Islam. Zoroastrianism is thought to have arisen in the late second millennium BC. (More on this in later pages)

The first undisputed burial approximately 150,000 years ago was performed by *Neanderthals*. In addition to funerals, *Neanderthals* made use of pigments, feathers, and even claws for abnormal bodily outlook. Architects also interpret *Neanderthal's* burial as suggestive of both belief in an afterlife and of ancestor worship. They also probably engaged in bear worship; but bear worship was not a major factor of *Paleolithic religion.*

## Religion in Human History

The first of the oldest surviving religious texts, *Pyramid Texts* was composed in ancient Egypt during 2494-2345 BC. During the *Minoan Civilization* developed in *Cete* in 2200 BC citizen worshipped a variety of goddesses. The oldest of them are Hindu Vedas (Scriptures). The *Rigveda* was composed during 1700 to 1100 BC. The Vedic age began in India after the collapse of the *Indus Valley Civilization* during 1500 BC.

The *Upanishads* (Vedic texts) were composed containing the earliest emergence of some of the central religious concepts of Hinduism, Buddhism and Jainism. The *Chandogya Upanishad* is compiled in 8th to 6th centuries of BC. During 6th to 5th centuries of BC, the first five books of Jewish *Torah* were probably composed. Closer to 1000 BC, Zoroastrianism flourished. The earliest Confucius' writing, *Shu Ching* appeared in 600 to 500 BC incorporating ideas of harmony and heaven.

*Mahavira*, 24th and last of *Tirthankara* of Jainism lived during 599 to 527 BC. *Buddha* from whom Buddhism originated was born in 551 BC. Confucius the founder of *Confucianism* was born in 399 BC. In 300 BC *Theravada Buddhism* was introduced in Sri Lanka by the venerable Mahinda. In 250 BC, Emperor Asoka propagated Buddhism in faraway countries. In 1400 BC, earliest grammar of Sanskrit literature was composed by *Panini.* In 100 BC to 500 AD, the *Yoga Sutra* of *Pathanjali* was composed.

Anthropologists estimate that at least 18,000 different gods, goddesses, and various animals or objects have been worshiped by humans since our species first appeared. Today at least 80% of the global population considers they are religious or spiritual in some forms. Humans think that spirituality offer something very tangible that enhanced procreation and survival. That is why, costly performances like gigantic pyramids to house the dead, blowing oneself up for the purpose of achieving paradise, or even sacrificing one's children as measures of devotion to one's deity had been practiced.

Religious beliefs, spirituality, and the need to worship a deity of some kind are undoubtedly durable traits.

Some gods were worshiped for very long periods and then they virtually disappeared from historical records. For example, the *Sun God Ra* was worshipped by many different customs for thousands of years and then completely disappeared. If historical proceeds hold value, many of the gods worshipped today will be forgotten and quickly replaced by others, as the evolution of humans and traits are differing as time passes on, and as evolution being progressive in all species including humanity. Certainly we are on our way to further evolvement that yet continues.

**What is in fact Religion or being Religious?**

The belief in and worship of a *Superhuman* Controlling Power, especially a personal god or gods is considered a religious activity. This approach essentially is inclusive of:

*Faith*
Strong belief in the doctrines of any religion, based on spiritual conviction rather than scientific or any established proof can be termed as faith. Faith can also be complete trust or confidence in someone or something be it a person or a system.

*Belief*
Belief is acceptance that something exists or is true, especially one without proof. The best example for this is god itself.

**Why do humans believe in Gods?**

Humans believe in some god or another because they believe that in communicating with a higher being, they begin to perceive evidence of that God's involvement and support in their lives. It also helps people regain some sense of control, or at least acceptance of what they undergo. Another motivational factor is an assurance of self-enhancement. Religion is priced, so is God.

## Major Religions of the present world

Hinduism is the world's oldest religion with roots and customs dating back more than 4,000 years. Today, with about 900 million followers, Hinduism is the third largest religion in the world after Christianity and Islam.

According to some estimates, there are roughly 4,200 religions, churches, denominations, religious bodies, faith groups, tribes, cultures, movements, ultimate concerns, all which at some points of time in the future will be countless. Mostly they are, Eastern religions, Middle Eastern religions, and Indigenous (ethnic, folks) religions. Also existed in the past were *Paganism, Animism, Totemic and Shamanism.*

Notions of gods arise in all human societies, from all-powerful and all-knowing deities to simple forest spirits. We will be discussing more about the major religions of the world in the next chapter.

## Human Generations

If we take each generation to be say 25 years in length, between the dawn of civilization and now, there had been just about 400 generation as per Wikipedia. This is an estimate of the civilized world, and not entire humanity's origin. It is because we do not have actual record of human origin and when it exactly began in a religious fashion,

## Human Civilizations

Following are distinct *Cradle of Civilizations* which have born and died in the world before us:

1. Mesopotamian
2. Assyrian
3. Maya
4. Roman Empire
5. Sumerian
6. Indus Valley
7. Achaemenidean
8. Hittites
9. Phoenician
10. Ancient Egyptian
11. Minoan
12. Inca Empire
13. Babylonian
14. Byzantine Empire
15. Old Chinese
16. Aztecs
17. Akkadian Empire
18. Indus River Valley
19. Carthage
20. Ancient Rome
21. Ancient Greece
22. Ancient Carthage
23. Mexican
24. Peruvian

## When did humans begin to worship Gods?

## Prehistoric evidence of religion

The exact time or period when humans first became religious remains unknown, however, research in evolutionary data or theology shows credible evidence of religious-cum-ritualistic behavior from around the *Middle Paleolithic Era* that is about 200,000 years ago!

The earliest surviving human made place of worship *Göbekli Tepe* is found in a hill sanctuary erected on the highest point of an elongated mountain ridge some 215 km north east of the *Town of Sanlirurfa* in the Southeastern Turkey, and what is the earliest surviving religious site, largely.

Prehistoric religion is the religious practice of prehistoric culture. Prehistory, the period before written records, make up the bulk of human experiences. Over 90% of human history occurred during the *Paleolithic* alone.

Prehistoric cultures spanned the globe and existed over two and half million years; their religious practices were many and varied, and the study of them difficult due to the lack of written records describing the details of their faiths.

**Neolithic Revolution**

The Neolithic Revolution was the critical transition that resulted in the commencement of agriculture, taking *Homo sapiens* from scattered groups of *hunter-gatherers* to farming villages and from there to technologically sophisticated societies with great temples and towers. *Neolithic or Agrarian revolution*, which established agriculture as the dominant lifestyle, occurred around 12,000 BC. This period also led to birth of kings and priests, who directed their labor forces. Their religious practices also changed to suit their then needs. *Neolithic religion* may have become more structural and centralized than the *Paleolithic* and possibly engaged in ancestor worship, both of one's individual ancestor and of the ancestor of entire groups, tribes, and settlements. One feature of *Neolithic religion* was the stone circles of the British Isles, of which the best-known today is *Stonehenge.*

## Bronze Age and Iron Age Religions

Bronze-age and Iron-age religions are understood in part through archeological records. Many Pagan faiths today are based on the pre-Christian practices of *Protohistoric* Bronze-age and Iron-age societies.

The question of when religion emerged in the evolving human psyche has sparked the curiosity of Paleontologists for decades. It is understood that *Hominins* had the cognitive capacity for spiritual belief. Religion was certainly present during the *Upper Paleolithic period*, dating to about 50,000 through 12,000 years ago, while religion in the Lower and Middle *Paleolithic* belongs to the realm of legend.

## Rituals

The first evidence of rituals appeared in the Hominin genus *Homo*, which emerged between 2 to 32 million years ago, and includes modern humans, their ancestors and closest relatives.

The lineage leading to anatomically modern humans originated around 500,000 years before the present day. Modern humans are classified taxonomically as *Homo sapiens.* The first undisputed burial, approximately 150,000 years ago, was performed by *Neanderthals.*

Some archeologists interpret *Neanderthal* burial as suggestions of both belief in an after-life and of ancestor worship. The evolutionary origin of religions and religious behavior is a field of evolutionary psychology, the origin of language and mythology, and cross-cultural comparison of the anthropology of religions. Some subjects of *Neolithic* religion include evidence of spirituality or culture behavior as in the *Upper Paleolithic* religion.

The exact period when humans first became religious remains unknown as we saw. However, details in evolutionary records show credible evidences of religious-cum-ritualistic behavior from around the *Middle-Paleolithic* era.

The early men did not judge anything with logic and reasoning but were governed by faith mostly due to fear of heavenly Super Powers and fear of natural disasters like earthquakes, thunder and lightning, landslides, avalanches and floods, heavy snowfalls, wildfires, dust storms, hurricanes, tropical storms, extreme climatically varying temperature, draughts, cyclones, wave surges, tornados, tsunamis, ice storms, sink holes, volcanic activities, heavy rains, even sometimes fear of animals and reptiles, over which they did not have any controls. They believed in a Super Human controlling them from above-heaven- and prayed to that power for their protection and safety. So, to say, such religious beliefs therefore originated from the human's fear of natural calamities of which they really had no idea and it continues even for a great number of people in this advanced age.

It means even today in the modern world with all its scientific and technological explanations and assurances against such nature's challenges, humans continue to fear God and worship in different ways for his protection, solace and peace of mind.

Apart from the enormous and countless religious believers, side by side, there are unbelievers, say, persons who are skeptical of any particular religion. Another common name for these unbelievers is *'Atheists'* who do not believe in any deity or any god, and are not followers of any religion.

## Why do most people choose to believe in God?

People still choose to believe in God mostly because they want a Supreme Power to defend them from the frightening world as we have seen the catastrophes list earlier. Trust in some Super Power which gives their life meaning, protection and purpose, something that stops death being the end of their being. In short, for them god is a hope and refuge for future life.

Religious beliefs and spiritual process have probably played the role in something like the success of civilizations. The most notable role is that a belief or faith in a spiritual or divine power that can add meaning and significance to many people's worldly lives, they believe.

In ancient civilizations, the role of religion was to form the social structures that developed individuals' spiritual quality. Religion is a set of beliefs concerning the big idea in the world involved in culture's behaviors and practices.

It is observed that religious practices are likely to help promote the well-being of individuals, families, and communities as a whole. Religious worships also lead to a reduction in the incidents of domestic abuses, crimes, substance abuses, and addictions. In addition, religious practices can increase physical and mental health, longevity, and education attainment. Most of all, religious participation in one or other group gives the feeling of inclusion and togetherness in society.

It is estimated that only 16% of people worldwide are not religious, but this still equates to approximately 1.2 billion individuals who find it difficult to reconcile the ideas of religion and its principles with what they know about the world from other sources like knowledge gained from science, technology, and philosophy, psychological and social fields.

Religious matters are a question that has played great thinkers for many centuries. *Karl Marx* for example, called religion the "opium of the people". *Sigmund Freud* felt that God was an illusion and worshippers were reverting to the childhood needs of security and forgiveness.

A more recent psychological explanation is the idea that our evolution has created a god-shaped hole or has given us a metaphorical *god engine* which can drive us to believe in a deity. Eventually, this hypothesis is that religion is a by-product of a number of cognitive and social adaptations which have been extremely important in human development.

**God**

In monotheistic thought, God is conceived of as the Supreme Being and creator and principal object of faith. God actually is conceived as being Omni-benevolent as well as having an eternal and necessary existence. God is most often held to be incorporeal, with said characteristics being related to conception of transcendence or immanence.

Some religions describe God without reference to gender-specific and gender based. God has been conceived as either personal or impersonal. In

*Theism*, God is the creator and sustainer of the universe, while in *Atheism* God is neither the creator nor the sustainer of the universe. In *Pantheism*, God is the universe itself. *Atheism* is an absence of belief in any god or deity, while *Agnosticism* deems the existence of God unknown or unknowable. God has also been conceived as the source of all moral obligations and the greatest conceivable extent. Many notable philosophers have developed arguments for and against the existence of God.

Each *Monotheistic* religion refers to its God using different names, some referring to cultural ideas about the god's identity and tributes. In ancient Egyptian *Atenism* (Aten religion or Amarna religion), possibly the earliest recorded *Monotheistic* religion, the deity was called *Aten* and proclaimed to be the one 'True Supreme Being' and creator of universe. In the Hebrew Bible, the titles of God include *'Elohim'* (God), *Adonai* (Lord) and others and the name *Yahweh* (Hebrew). The names Yahweh and *Jehovah*, possible vocalizations of *YHWH*, are used in Christianity. In Judaism some of the Hebrew titles of God are considered holy names. In the Christian doctrines of *'Trinity'*, or God coexists in three 'persons' called the Father, the Son and Holy Spirit. In Islam, the title God (Allah in the Arabic language) is often used as a name, while Muslims also use a multitude of other titles for God which are collectively known as *Asmaa al-Husna*. In Hinduism, *Brahma* is often considered a Monistic concept of God. In Chinese religion, *Shangri'* is conceived as the *Progenerator* (first ancestor) of the universe, intrinsic to it and constantly bringing order to it.

Other names of some Gods include *'Baha'i'* in the Baha'i faith, *'Waheguru'* in Sikhism, *'Ahure Mazda'*
18

in Zoroastrianism, and '*Sang Hyang Widhdi Wasa*' in Balinese Hinduism.

Historically in some parts of India, people followed *Sharna Dharma* and worshipped Nature, particularly trees. There are also people who worship animals and reptiles like, rats and snakes, etc. In short, we see evidence of people worshipping anything that is believed to have Divine Power over them. Gods are innumerable, yesterdays and today, and probably tomorrows also as long as humans remain unaware of the reality of their standards and strengths but depend on beliefs mostly followed in continuity of their parents or ancestors.

There are cases of motivational reasons for religious belief and adherence to religious groups. People who are socially isolated tend to have more religious faiths, perhaps allowing them to feel they are not truly alone. Such people are inclined to show more than what they really are religious and opt to be in the forefront of matters concerning to religious group activities, just like that. Likewise, people who face chances of death are more likely to express excess faith in God and an afterlife too. There is an old saying that "There are no atheists on the battle field".

Furthermore, faith in God increases when situations become uncomfortable as in the case of natural disasters. Believing that God has a plan to help people in detrimental circumstances brings about some sense of emotional control or at least acceptance of reality.

Another motivational factor is self enhancement. Say, if you live in a society where religion and faith is priced, it is in your best interest to say you believe, whether you totally do or not. Religion and faith, for some preachers and celebrants are important, irrespective of whether they truly adhere closely to their belief because it is a way they can make a living. There are so many religious celebrants who adore *borrowed feathers* to live pretentious and enjoy life.

There are also solid factors that influence the degrees of religious belief within societies. Japan and Western Europe are some countries where scientists call *post religious* because of negligible number of people who believe and follow religious ways there today.

Throughout history, people's faith and their attachment to religious institutions have transformed widely. Before Buddha, Jesus and Muhammed there was Zoroaster some 3500 years ago, in Bronze-age Iran. He had a vision of the supreme God. A thousand years later came Zoroastrianism, the world's first great Monotheistic religion, the official faith of the mighty Persian Empire, with its Fire Temples attended by millions of adherents. A thousand years after that, sadly the empire collapsed, and the followers of Zoroaster were persecuted and converted to the new faith of their conquerors, Islam.

Today after another 1500 years, Zoroastrianism is a dying faith, its Sacred Flames tended over fewer worshipers. This could well be the fate of many of today's religions in years to come like many other religions once flourished but died out sooner or later.

**Origin of all major religions**

The *history* of religion refers to the written record of human religious feelings, thoughts and ideas. This period of religious history is known to us with the invention of writing about 6,000 years ago.

The *prehistory* of religion involves the study of religious beliefs that existed prior to the advent of written records. These are invariably obtained from the archeological records, and cave or earthen excavation findings but do not have strong proof or authority except mere perceptions especially with regard to their age. The entire human history of yester years are having the same fate, nothing authentically proven other than speculations. Even today we unearth historically important articles and paintings and try to establish their age or period of creation.

Chapter 4

# Major World Religions

It was stated earlier that there are almost 4,200 religions and sub-religions in the world today according to some estimates and inclusive of various churches, denominations, religious bodies, faith groups, tribes, cultures, movements etc. Perhaps this figure is just indicative as more and more faith groups are flourishing all around the world. They all worship mostly different gods, giving us the idea, what Religion exactly is, how unsubstantial the count be.

The most prominent of them are:

1.  **Christianity** (1st century AD)

Christianity is an Abrahamic, monotheistic religion based on the birth, life, teachings, death and resurrection of Jesus of Nazareth believed to be the *Son of God*. Christianity began in the 1st century AD after Jesus died and was resurrected. Starting as a small group of Jewish people in Judea, it spread quickly throughout the Roman Empire and to the whole world. The religion was adopted as State Religion by Emperor Constantine giving a boost for it to spread all over Europe and in the rest of the world. Today Christianity is the largest religion of the world considering the number of its adherents (31.11%).

*The Bible* is their Holy Book containing mainly two parts, the Old Testament and the New Testament.

## 2.   Islam (7th Century AD)

Islam is another Abrahamic monotheistic religion teaching that Prophet Muhammad is a messenger of *Allah* (God). *Islam* means surrender/submission to *Allah*. It is the world's second largest religion with 1.9 billion followers, or 24.9% of the world's population, known as Muslims. Muslims make up a majority of the population in 47 countries. *The Quran* is their Holy Book.

## 3.   Hinduism (Between 2,300 BC & 1,500 BC)

Hinduism is the world's oldest organized religion, in fact a way of life. In Sanskrit it is called *Sanadhana Dharma. Brahma* is the Hindu God of Creation. He is also known as *Prajapathi*, the primeval first God. *Brahma* is the Supreme in the Triad of Great Hindu Gods which include *Siva* and *Vishnu*. The four *Vedas* of Hinduism was compiled between 15th and 5th centuries BC. The roots and customs of Hinduism are considered the oldest dating back to 4,000 years. Today, with 900 million followers, Hinduism is the third-largest religion (15%). The primary sacred texts of Hindus are *Vedas*.

## 4.   Judaism (9th to 5th century BC);

Judaism is an Abrahamic, Monotheistic, and Ethnic religion comprising the collective religious, cultural, and legal tradition and civilization of the Jewish people, originated in the 1st millennium BC; 20th to 18th century BC in Judah; Mesopotamia. It had its roots as an organized religion in the Middle East during the Bronze-Age. An ancient Egyptian faith called '*Atenism*' disappeared in the 14th century BC., whereas Judaism originated in the kingdoms of Israel and Judah around the 9th century BC, and morphed into its current form in 6th century BC. Judaism is followed by 11 to 14 million people. The Jewish sacred text is called the *Tanoak* or the 'Hebrew Bible'.

## 5. **Jainism** (8th to 2nd Century BC)

In succession of faiths came Christianity (1st Century AD and Islam (7th century AD). Jainism came in 8th to 2nd Century BC.

Jainism has fairly obscure origins. Jainism is traditionally known as *Jain Dharma*. It is one of the oldest Indian religions. Its followers believe in *Tirthankara,* omniscient preachers of Jain faith, whose defining characteristics are marked by asceticism and self-discipline. Historically known are two Gurus, *Tirthankara Parshvanatha* (8th century BC) and *Mahavira* (599-527 BC). Yet Jainism archeologically dates back to the second century BC, Jains said to number 6 to 7 million worldwide.

## 6. **Confucianism** (6th to 5th Century BC)

Confucianism should invariably be traced back to one man, the Chinese politician, teacher and philosopher *Confucius* (551 to 479 BC), who was of a scholarly tradition dating back to an earlier golden age. It is an ancient Chinese belief system focusses on the importance of personal ethics and morality named after its mentor Confucius. After Confucius's death, the tradition has gone through various periods of popularity and unpopularity in China, and remains one of the leading influences of modern Chinese folk religions. Strict Confucians are said to number about

6 million. The religion is more or less confined to China and its people around.

### 7.   **Buddhism** (6th to 5th Century BC)

Buddhism is one of the world's largest religions and originated 2,500 years ago in India. *Siddhartha Gautama* or *Buddha* was the founder and leader of his own monastic order – one of the many sects – known as *Sramana.* His teachings began to be codified shortly after his death, and continue to be followed by at least 400 million people in various countries (7%). Buddhists believe that human life is prone of suffering, and that meditation, spiritual and physical labor and good behavior are the ways to achieve enlightenment. *Buddha* asked not to build his statues after his death, but all around the world Buddha statues are prevalent, bedded by his devotees. The *Tripitaka* is the Holy Book of Buddhism.

### 8.   **Taoism** (6th to 4th century BC)

Tao-Te-Ching (*Sage Laozi*) has been a contemporary of Confucius in the 4th century BC. The religion evolved from a strand of traditional Chinese folk religion. It is a religion and a philosophy from ancient China. Taoism holds that humans and animals should live in balance with the *Tao,* or the universe. Taoists believe in spiritual immortality, where the spirit of the body joins the universe after death. Today an estimated 170 million Chinese claim affiliation with Taoism, with 12 million following it strictly. Their Chinese classic text *Tao-Te-Ching* written by *Laozi* is followed as their Holy Book.

## 9. Shintoism (3rd century BC to 8th century AD)

Shintoism is a direct descendent of the Animistic folk religion of the *Yayoi,* whose culture spread throughout Japan in 3rd century BC. Shinto is *Polytheistic* and revolves around the *kami,* supernatural entities believed to inhabit all things. Today the faith is unified accent of ancient Japanese mythology and followed by vast majority of country's population. The Holy Books of Shinto are the *Kojiki* or Records of Ancient Matters (712 AD) and the *Nihon-gi* or Chronicles of Japan (720 AD). These books are compilations of ancient myths and traditional teachings that had previously been passed down orally.

## 10. Sikhism (5th century BC)

Sikhism or *Sikh* is an Indian religion originated in the Punjab region of India around the end of the 15th century AD. Sikhism is one of the youngest of the major religions and the world's 5th largest organized religion with about 320 million followers at the beginning of 21st century. Meditation upon and devotion to the Creator, Truthful Living and Service to Humanity are its merits. Sikhs are meant to uphold the values of honesty, compassion, generosity, humility, integrity, service, and spirituality on a daily basis. The Sikhs call their faith *Gourmet* (The Way of the Guru). According to Sikh tradition, Sikhism was established by Guru Nanak (1469-1539 AD) and subsequently led by a succession of nine other Gurus. *Grant Sahib* is the sacred scripture of Sikhism. It is a collection of nearly 6,000 hymns of the Sikh Gurus and various early and medieval saints of different religions and castes.

### **11. Zoroastrianism** (6$^{th}$ Century BC)

Zoroastrianism or *Mazdayasna* is one of the world's oldest continuously-practiced religions, the ancient religion of Iran (*Persia*) based on the teachings of the Iranian-speaking prophet *Zoroaster.* It is the oldest religion surfaced in the Middle East. It has a dualistic cosmology of good and evil and an eschatology which predicts the ultimate conquest of evil by good. Zoroastrians offer their prayers in Fire Temple. It is estimated that there are about 100,000 to 200,000 Zoroastrians worldwide. *Zend-Avesta* is the sacred book of Zoroastrianism containing its cosmogony, law, and liturgy, the teachings of the *Prophet Zoroaster (Zarathustra).*

*NB: Yazdanism* (Cult of Angels) is a faith which have evolved from a mix of Islam and a Hurrian Precursor to the Zoroastrian faith)

### **Others**

There are numerous faith cults around the world which have very little followers, some surviving and many disappeared. Every faith holds the name of a god of their choice and description. We are not following their ways and goals and as these faiths are mostly belonging to some particular sects or regions and are neither world religions or of any significance to this volume.

### **World Religious Populations (2020)**

As said earlier there are about 4200 religions and sub-religions in our world. Some of them are itemized below, based on the strength of their followers:

Christianity;   31.11%, Islam; 24.90%, Unaffiliated; 15.58%, Hinduism; 15.16%, Buddhism; 6.62%, Folk

Religions; 5.61%, other religions; 0.79%, (which include: Judaism; Zoroastrianism; Baha'i faith; Taoism; Shinto; Confucianism; Rastafari; Chinese Folk Religions; Cao Dai; Modern Paganism; Tenrikyo; Wicca; Traditional African Religions; Protestantism; Caodaism; Gnosticism;) etc.

## Decline of Religions

On our observation globally, most religions began to decline suddenly or gradually. In fact, the process did not happen overnight. The major religions had presented a global resurgence in 21st century. However, the most dramatic shift away from religions took place among the American public. The trend seems to happen virtually among all other high-income countries. In short religiosity has been declining more rapidly in the US than in most other countries. Although some religious conservatives warn that the retreat from faith will lead to a collapse of social cohesion and public morality, the evidence does not support the claim. Surprisingly it appears that concentrates that are less religious actually tend to be less corrupt or have lower murder rates than religious ones. It is almost 10% higher in religious states. It is also noticed that crime and religiosity tend to be high in poor countries.

In early Agrarian Society, when most people lived just above the survival level, religion may have been the most effective way to maintain order and cohesion. But as traditional religiosity declined an equally strong set of moral norms seems to be emerging to fill the void.

As societies develop from Prehistoric-to agrarian-to Industrial-to knowledge based, growing existential security tends to reduce the importance of religion in people's lives and people became less obedient to traditional religious leaders and institutions, as per Prof. Ronald F Ingle Hart, Political Science emeritus at the University of Michigan, the author of *Religion's Sudden Decline*.

# Chapter 5

# Impact of Religions on Human Behaviors

### Scientific Vs religious perspectives

In the previous chapters we have comprehended the statistics on various leading religions and their presence in the world as of now. Now let us evaluate and study whether or not these religions are likely to survive and if yes, how long based on the comparison of fate of religions earlier emerged and died out.

This book "To be or Not to be Religious" just echoes genuine thoughts of an adequately free-thinking and inquisitive human brain of 21$^{st}$ century in line with the reliable and undisputable genuine facts that the entire progress of the world and humanity had just happened as we see today mainly because of recent science and technological developments when we compare the old world in which our esteemed predecessors lived and advanced to this date step by step as if from darkness to brightness very bravely facing many odds on their earnest to survival this far simultaneously weighing old notions and beliefs existed prior to their era since the beginning of human evolution if we consider fairly.

And it is sadly very much true and obvious through history that it is just religions a major factor that caused lot of distress and bloodshed to mankind through wars and hatred, than any other natural perils

31

like catastrophes of many natures. Fear of the unknown super power believed existing above in the heavens, is what triggered in the world, lightening, thunder, heavy rains, earthquakes, landslides, plague etc. as cause of extinctions and suffering in the world, an idea created in the minds of the barbaric early humans was root cause for all these havocs. That is how godly beliefs, identified as religion originated with the early helpless prehistoric humans lived in the wilderness and caves then. It grew to such great and grave situation slowly but firmly as of today in all different religions throughout the world in different parts in different stages of human existence. And, the establishment called religions succeeded in promoting that fear in the minds of people by and large and thus reaping the benefit of holding humanity under fear of punishment from almighty god - this far, though it is an hypothesis without any proof or real merit as considered in the modern world. This very fact is obvious from the natural trend of large scale shift of people of late from idealism to realism.

**Future of Religions**

What would be the future of Religions and by that of gods is just speculation at this stage from the trends shifting of the world. History indicates the growth and fall of several religions and faiths in our good old sweet world so far. Of them most important religions of the past what faded away, their temples and statues vanished, their gods barely remembered are namely, Sumerian, Babylonian, Assyrian, Egyptian, Greek, Samaritanism, Vedism, Olmec religion, Ashurism, Manichaeism, Tengriism, Mithraism and Roman religion, Germanic and Norse Religion, Mayan religion, Minaon religion, Atenism, Canaanite religion, Finish Paganism, all according to a report in 2021, of which Canaanite Polytheism or Bal worship consolidated its many gods to become Judaism that survives today. Bahai, Zoroastrianism, Ali-lllahism, Druze, Yazidi, Mandeanism, Gnosticism, Shabakism etc are some names of religions previously heard of and still being practiced in some parts of the world in some form or other. In all, religions of our ancestors appeared and disappeared one by one during the passage of time, leaving behind a lot of history about those civilizations from which we had lot to learn.

Logically, what we observe and worship earnestly today may also vanish in future, perhaps faster as humanity advances faster than ever on the basis of scientific and technological foundation. Holland is one example where officially they have declared absence of any god. But still a minute part of them believes in some religions including Christianity.

In countries like India, instead of focusing our efforts and resources to come out of the pit of poverty, we seem channeling all our efforts for promoting religion, especially one against another only to grab vote banks. Such is our disorderly culture. It sure is failure of a clean democracy although we praise ourselves an epitome of peoples rule. Religion is a major tool in the hands of some dirty short sighted politicians to cause split and disharmony between and among various religious groups, intended mainly for their own survival or growth. Even modern educated lot is tool in the hands of politicians.

As it was portrayed in my earlier book "Major religions of the world", the following present religions are still surviving and being practiced in large or small scale in and around the world. They are: Hinduism, Jainism, Buddhism, Sikhism, Confucianism, Taoism, Shintoism, Judaism, Sorsahtranism (parse), Islam, and Christianity. The fate of these religions also to be seen as time goes on. In Europe and many western countries where Christianity was at its helm during the immediate past is now slowing down fast and we have to imagine the fate of the rest of the religions following suit from the trend of the time.

In the words of Indian spiritual Guru of yester years Acharya Rajneesh (Osho), who preached an eclectic doctrine, Eastern Mysticism and individual devotion on advanced thought lines, "Gods as commonly enumerated as a person Almighty in all religions are to be dropped in favor of real godliness and religions have to disappear in favor of religiousness" is very consequential.

We have seen that all the past great and not so great religions of the world had died out over ages and that stands a convincing question to be reckoned with; is there a creator for this heterogeneous world or not? It is obvious that man's fear of the unknown resulted in the creation of the super power called god, and one by one many gods thus were created and worshipped in various situations and periods all over the world. In such case it is just the acceptable logical conclusion that gods were created by man for his own needs beyond his capacity to meet with. Age old beliefs died out beyond the scope of revivals because they were created by immature minds and now became irreverent for our times, as we have come of that age. Similarly, some of our existing beliefs also got to be modified to suit our times, thus freeing ourselves from the dogmas of yester years, that only will help us to look forward to a bright and sensible tomorrow.

34

Religious frontrunners try keeping us chained to fearful punishments for man's errors committed knowingly or unknowingly to control our senses. This trend has to end for upbeat future of humanity. Sadly, we are so much attached to the old norms of fear of gods as we feel comfort and security having them for our protection during challenging times and so refrain from leaving them behind or even to think of a situation without the support and guidance of god because we have always hurdles of life on our journey. The Genevan philosopher and writer of political philosophy Jean-Jacques 'Rousseau' had stated thus, "Man is born free but always remains in chain". This 'chain' is at times political and always religious in nature in many cases throughout the human evolution from the prehistoric to this date. Man has to break these chains and come into terms of reality because only then he can have a profound tomorrow probable devoid of religious hatred, completion, and tug-o-war of many sorts.

Now the serious question is that, will it be possible for humanity to drop gods from their life on earth till such time he has no fear of his life which could only be acquired from real knowledge because, he had been so much acquainted with a life with gods which provided him comforts at times of difficulties, a pillar to lean on, consolations and convenience with regard to this or that. Similarly, clinging to a god or many gods and one or more religions surely gave him a sort of identity and social status in most common areas. Therefore, dropping them from his day to day life becomes unthinkable and all the more frightening. Till such time man converge this capability, the merchants of religions will do their business of instigating the weak men to follow the ideals of divinity and faith of this or that kind whether or not real spirituality is counted and maintained.

The mind wants to hold on to the known and familiar life pattern because of a trodden path he created as the mind is always orthodox and conventional. Therefore the mind sticks to the past and take him forward to the future in the same rhythm. He does not have the willingness to think differently and think in any challenging way which results in a fight between mind and life itself. It is said, "Those who choose life instead of the mind are the salt of the earth". But truly the question of this choice is selective and decisive.

So, what is in store for religions in the future is the million dollar question for which no definite answer is available with the author other than speculations. The common trend we see around the world in denouncing religions and their observances in the progressive interest of society, a trend seems acquiring momentum on the simple and most important aspect that religions are not progressive in their ideas corresponding to the progress man made in very many regions of his existence such as science, technology, communication in particular, ways of advanced social thinking in the universal interests, hygiene, transportation, peace on earth, universal brotherhood, etc. It had been the case in the past that when one religion collapse another one will rise in some other form and pattern and try to stay with the weak minded, man always are, thus preserve its existence till such time all men think differently.

So, we can expect to see sea-change in humanitarian values and corresponding transformation in their life around the world that sees future for their people and nations. So, to say, those who drop gods for godliness and religions for religiousness in reality should have great value added life on earth, which itself is a challenge for most. And, if that is possible and fully attained, they are the people of the future.

## Uncertainties about religious future

Human life from its very origin is an ongoing adventure, a continuing exploration towards the bright future of mankind but still unknown and incomplete for sure even at this point of time in our 21$^{st}$ century. The violence and barbaric occurrences against mankind even today tell us that there is no guarantee of peaceful coexistence of humanity in the near future and wars and terrorism would cause innumerable destructions for mankind as it was existing in the past and in the present and this is a sure fact of concern for those who wish to live and progress peacefully on earth.

In honest and impartial opinions, even if a handful of religions continue to exist in the future in some form, before it vanishes sooner or later as in the past, it will not be focused on varied ritual practices as of our predecessors or of the contemporary. It will be a new ideology of coexisting on mutual acceptance and forgiveness what is needed by the liberal humans of this and future generations. It will be a religion that will not be confined by any dogma. It will not supply the philosophy and worshipping pattern of any present religion, but will give us the vision of a different dimension based on reality. This alone will stop people thinking of fighting, standing for just one path for salvation of humanity, but many ways of harmony and coexistence in the best way possible resulting in a better society without teachings and interference of any particular religion. Whether such an excellence in social integration can be called a religion or not is uncertain at this point of time.

Current religious views are of very old pattern fitted to those times they were born and that is what costing the conflicts and perplexity in society today. We can show a hundred examples for this comparing with the views of the modern world. Those procedures ought to be modified to suit the advanced generation, but none do so. A vast majority of religious people are reluctant to modify their beliefs and views in relation to their genuine scientific knowledge attained through ages and lead a life accordingly mainly in fear of consequential punishments from god they trust. Religious establishments and leaders are mainly responsible for this attitude. For example, we know the destiny of American inventor Thomas Alva Edison. His invention of electric light bulb is one of the greatest gifts to the world when we look at it from reality. But he was found guilty of transforming god who was believed to have created darkness into light, by then Christian authorities and excommunicated him from the church labelling him as anti-god. Similar is the case of Nicholas Copernicus from Poland who found that the earth rotates upon its axis and revolves around the sun which was against the then belief that the earth is flat and sun revolves around the earth giving us day and night. He was also restricted by then church saying he contradict the religious theories and norms. However, the Italian Astronomer Galileo Galilei confirmed that earth is a spherical body that rotates around its own axis and simultaneously circles the sun. He was also reprimanded by the then church standing on its terms that the earth is a flat body and sun rotates it from west to east. All these religious views till then were utterly wrong and were false age old concepts but the advent of science proved them wrong. There could be more such surprises to be revealed before our eyes as man reached deepest parts of oceans and farthest outer world already.

So is the belief of heaven and earth. At least in the Abrahamic faiths of Christianity, Islam and some schools of Judaism as well as Zoroastrianism, heaven is the realm of afterlife where good actions in the previous life on earth are rewarded for eternity. Hell is the opposite where bad ones are punished and thrown in. Heaven is therefore, in many religions, the abode of god or the gods, as well as of angels, deified humans, the blessed dead and other celestial beings. The learned men of the world today know these are hum bucks and rotten ideas created to control the innocent multitude and show them a path of excellence to lead a better life on earth so that they attain benefit later. These philosophies are still prevalent before us to follow if one sticks to the religion he or she belongs.

Even more clearly based on understanding of scriptures such as Revelation 14:1-4 in Holy Bible it seems Jehovah's Witnesses believe that exactly 144,000 faithful Christians go to heaven to rule with Christ in the kingdom of God. Don't know the fate of the rest in the world amounting to several crores of humans, past dead, present living and of future until the end of world.

There are many religions who believe that one's status in the afterlife is consequences of one's conduct during earthly life. Whatever, none returned from heaven to tell us the real story but we continue to export the souls to heaven. Our forefathers who preached the heaven and hell might have only thought of instigating the sort of fear in generations to do well and live harmoniously on earth in anticipation of having a place in heaven in the afterlife. It has become a major business for livelihood of the preachers and teachers now leading or misleading population to nowhere. Religious leaders generally are blessed with lavish and comfortable sometimes exorbitant life on earth whether or not they succeed in exporting souls to heaven.

## Philosophical reflection of religious thoughts

The real question now is whether philosophical reflection of religious thoughts of yester years still holds value in the modern scientific and robotic artificial intelligence induced technological world of 21$^{st}$ century? What do we get to do for a neat and wise fruitful and progressive life on earth where we are placed now, whatever the afterlife be. Humans belong to the *Sapiens* family or 'wise monkeys' of the past as science tell us. That is why we are able to question why we are doing what we do, a method of intelligent philosophical capability. It is time now we connect our religious thoughts to this parameter and ask us whether our belief in particular religion of the old school is wise action or not. And, this exploration will give right answer to every action of our life. If one decides to continue with his customary style go ahead or else modify to the new and metaphysical ideas and live a different acceptable life pattern, all new fitting today's world.

The ability to think for oneself gives rise to intelligent questions on our existence which comes up quite spontaneously in mind; such as: what is real; is the material and tangible world real or reality to be found somewhere else beyond? Are we confused at this point as to either believe in science and live accordingly or follow any suitable religious paths of great traditions of faith? We may not realize whether we are seeking metaphysical or epistemological answers to our wavering mind. Precisely that is our great confusion today for every thinking mind. Those who do not bother to think wisely enough can easily follow the line of his or her traditions and still find solace without causing any mental agony or confusion because for him or her religious adherence give satisfaction and solace of all sorts.

## The Purpose of life

George Wilhelm Friedrich Hagel was a German philosopher, one of the most influential figures of German idealism who believed that "Philosophy could go to the roofs of a culture, truth of the absolutes that it embodies". The echoes of philosophy help the society to comprehend its strength and weakness in terms of religious or political characteristics. What does it mean to be moral or ethical and how does one judge whether a human action is right or wrong and questions which man articulate on the basis of religions and their teachings or on common prevailing trends. Is the human existence itself is meaningless as we see great lots of sufferings, grief and misery among populations produced by believers and non-believers all over the world from the beginning of humans till date. What is the purpose of our life facing all these to survive and why not gods have control over them and let us live peacefully so long we live and allow us enjoy, just enjoy.

"Philosophical wisdom may come late for the above questions, but these questions loom large at the back of our minds, all human minds sometime or other especially on everyday challenges in life", contends Prof. Thelma Z. Levine, an American Philosopher and writer. They come to the forefront in moments of deep personal crisis or in the face of an external sudden event of a catastrophe like earthquake or a war, when one despairs and one's faith in a particular belief system is shaken. We all should ask these fundamental questions: what is real and valuable, what is true and just and the new generations should shape their minds to believe and follow them accordingly than resting in old philosophies and theological teachings which may not fit for the present generation for peaceful community life and co-existence, other than having spent a life after cooked up spirituality than reality, achieving nothing.

It is therefore reiterated in the words of Bertrand Arthur William Russel that "From ancient times till now, all sorts of development in the world had happened due to the ushering in of science and technology and the main reason for all distress to mankind including several wars fought all over the world had caused due to contribution of religious involvement and initiation and on the whole that amount to much more than natural calamities."

## Liberalism by choice

To attain peaceful co-existence in this world we share with all others we should learn to live leaving behind vices and ill-attachments. Also, we should embrace realization, transformation and purification of our minds by imbibing and inculcating good virtues not essentially taught by religions of any kind, old or new because these are common ethical life models and we don't need any religion to instill them in us.

The author would advise to respect all religions as long as they exist, let all people enjoy the choices and teachings of their religions and let other people join them and live their way to their liking, that is liberalism by choice. A state like India cannot patronize or profess any particular religion with its secularistic norms defined in the constitution so that no one will be able to engender hatred in the name of a religion or faith nor compel others to follow. Everyone should only engage in furthering better relationship and not hatred in the name of religion. Honestly, it is better to have no religion if the very purpose of humanity is not perceived in its abstract sense.

To Be or Not To Be Religious is one of the most emotional dilemma man faces today in the scholarly world and the answer is, be religious if you have a weaker mind and you are in need of a pillar of trust to go on in life like a creeper that requires support of a stronger tree to grow and survive on the face of windy and troublesome whether and bear fruit than perishing. Strong and capable and all the more intelligent minds do not require this support for their existence as far as it recognize that gods and faiths are manmade obligations through generations and it ended by now as just a means for many for their life support and not essential for those who can face turbulences of this world and still able to live on one's own will and strength of one's inner mental ability. To conclude, it is all in the state of your/my mind, to be or not to be religious. Wherever and whenever humans are weak, let surviving religions strengthen him and when he is able to come off this fear and insecurity let religious influences on him vanish….as it had been occurring thus since the origin of mankind and fate of religions he created. Perhaps it could be nature's destiny.

# Chapter 6

# Advantages and Disadvantages of Religiousness in the Present Age

Subject 'Religion' is a very vast and puzzling topic. Many studies have documented the benefits and detriments of religious involvements and emphasis on human populations from very olden times. At the present age too we notice it in front of our eyes.

Detailed and systematic studies in a nut shell are that highly religious people tend to be healthier, live longer, and have higher levels of subjective well-being. That is one major valid view. However it is conditional. In fact while religious involvement offers clear benefits to many, it may also be detrimental to some. Now the curious question is, if religious involvements are beneficial as a principle, how come many people in and around today's progressive world abandoning their religions and become non-religious or atheists, as a pattern we notice around.

Religious people often claim that their belief system supplies their life with meaning, moral guidance, being in a social structure as well as a sense of comfort in harsh and challenging world. Religious community living proves this point right for many believers.

However, the arguments of non-believers in any religion appear more logical and sensible. It is based on challenging Supernatural ideas rather than science. Religions before and present always leave room for conflicts within believers, restrict freedom of thought, often encourages bigotry against minorities, create unscrupulous leaders and preachers usually looking forward for their own profits and purposes including leadership benefits, standing as obstacles in the way of progress holding on to very old norms and practices, encourage suffering in this world anticipating a wonderful life after death, etc. Religions are considered having Utopian thinking as they are man-made arrangements than divine, and so on.

First of all, religions; all religions, are based on the fallacy that the universe was created and operates according to Supernatural rules and forces rather than proven scientific laws. Today's man clearly differentiate tales of miracles, appearances of unearthly beings, existence of devils, all as perverted human creations and have no backing from science.

Our past history of religions mapped many wars and conflicts throughout the world from many centuries earlier and even today they behave as enemies for one thing or other while claiming the apostles of peace and humanity. Millions of people have laid down their lives in the name of religions alone, and the evil is still continuing in most parts of the world. A world without conscientious stigma has no reasons to fight each other when claiming that they wish to establish peace on earth which is not comprehensible. This is because devout believers often believe or made to believe that their particular creed is the only acceptable one and that all the others are either false or dangerous, especially threat to their existence. Means, as long as many religions exist there will be religious rebellion and wars among them that is definite naturally.

Vigorously religious people seem to have inadequate brains or at least one sided. They blindly follow the injections of their spiritual leaders without thinking on the way they should be using their brains. It is because either they are not allowed to think their way or restricted of their freedom of thoughts when it comes to independent religious thoughts. They are encouraged by the idea that fundamental answers are fixed according to the rule books they follow and that can be found as stipulated by their priests and leaders. In short, a culture of unquestionable loyalty is encouraged on the followers, or fear of divine punishments is enforced on the followers. People are scared to raise any question against patriarchal teachings. Such is the condition dissenters are socially ostracized or punished through blasphemy laws. Even violence in extreme circumstances is outstretched in certain cases. Practically, what we see around is that unscrupulous religious leaders use their religious authority and status to enrich themselves by accumulating wealth, live lavishly and even venture into misdemeanors as if they are unquestionable. And the lay-men simply accept it or remain silent.

One more thing is very certain; religions only interested in holding humanity backwards. As we have seen earlier, during medieval times scientific inventions and discoveries almost grounded to a standstill and scientists were shoddily treated by the rulers because their findings obstructed or stood against the religious beliefs and teachings of those periods. It was after the arrival of secularism in the free-thinking age things really began to move forward.

## Psychological Impacts

All existing religions can be said to be instigating fear to intimidate dissenters of god's punishments and maintain ultimate power with them by granting pardon for sins. We have several stories of apostates persecuted or killed blasphemers imprisoned, or at least failed believers threatened with hell as their destiny.

Most religions are Utopian by nature; promising flourishing after-life after worldly existence and even persuades people to undergo sufferings in this world so that they get eternal pleasurable life after death. In short religions practice and encourage idealist ideas and promise great achievements, but in reality such life leads to frustrations and disappointment among followers. But they stick to their religions in the brighter hope and illusion of great opportunities, a mass psychological escapism of all times through generations.

There are plenty of people who are neither religious nor atheists, but apathetic. The existence of one god or many gods do not make a big difference when it comes to morality and ethics in our midst. Morality still survives without the help of gods and ethics continue to subsist as long as people are educated as well understand other people's life situations and humanity in its practicality.

48

## Timeline of Religions

Man is by nature religious or superstitious, either of two. There is evidence to prove that man believed in spirits and supernatural forces for over hundreds of thousands of years. However, these Prehistoric or Stone Age religions had no organized or monolithic beliefs or dogmas. Instead everyone was free to believe in his own beliefs and to practice his own 'religion' without applying common sense or logic.

The beliefs of these religions were transmitted horizontally between contemporaries as well as vertically from one generation to the next by word of mouth and some practices. In the process their religious and cultural characteristics or ideas mutated and evolved with each transmission so much so that the gods and spirits worshipped in one generation was completely unrecognizable after a few generations of memetic mutation and evolution. Everyone was free to believe in his or her own gods and to practice it as they thought fit. Even the same person could change his or her own beliefs and practices as he pleased as many times during his or her lifetime. In short, in those days religion was a personal thing and there was no political dimension or compulsions to it as we experience in today's modern world or head hunting to force believe in any majority religion. Then man turned to letters about 5000 or more years ago.

## Progression of Religions

Mostly, if not all of man's technical innovations were developed for commercial purposes and literacy was no different. Thus the first pieces of writing were for keeping track of commercial transactions especially during agricultural era. It was a matter of time before this literacy was extended to philosophy, fiction, nonfiction and stories including myths and religions. This resulted in two kinds of religions – religions without any books called natural religions and religions based on written books which we may call religions of the books.

One of the first books to be written for religious purposes was the Vedas. This forms the basis of Brah-manic Hinduism, one of the most structured old religions in the world. In contrast non-Brah-manic Hinduism practiced by the majority of Hindus is a natural religion which goes on mutating and evolving like Stone Age religions with new personal gods such as Sathya sai Baba, Matha Amruthananda Mayi, and a lot of such men and women appearing and disappearing with time and place.

Besides the Vedas, other religious books came into vogue, books such as the Avesta, The Brahmanas, The Ramayana, The Gita, The Sutra, The Tantras, The Upanishads, The Buddhism, The Samhita, The Agama, The Guru Granth Sahib, The Tao Te Ching, The Bhagavata Purana, The Iliad, The Epic of Gilgamesh, The Torah, The Bible comprising of the Old Testament and The New Testament, The Quran, and so forth. These books are essentially of Bronze Age, like Eastern Asian Religions, Iranian Religions, Indian Religions, Abrahamic religions, Pre-Columbian Americas religion, Ethnic religions, anything. One of the last of these religious books to be propagated is the Mormon Bible written in the 19th century with the life of Jesus set in an American background. It may be of interest to note that the Mormons are the fastest growing denomination of Christianity in America as of in this generation.

We have seen how before the arrival of these written scriptures and myths, there was a constant mutation and evolution of religious memes, both horizontally and vertically. However, with the writing down of religious dogmas, myths and scriptures, these books of the religions fossilized or calcified giving these religions no room for further mutation and evolution. What is more, each of these religions of the books claimed that their book alone was god-inspired and that all other were blasphemous abominations against the true god? However, since none of these religions of the book were in a position to provide any evidence for their claims of divine authority or infallibility, they began to resort to violence to prove that their religion alone was the true divine religion and even this day this violence continues though nobody is able to prove their claim but keep claiming.

In addition, though writing down the myths and scriptures of religions led to the stability of these religions, in the absence of any evidence to bolster up the veracity of these claims of the religions, they led to different interpretations of the same myths and scriptures of the same book. The result was an explosion of sects and denominations of the same religions based on the different interpretations of the same book. Thus in Christianity alone, there are over 50,000 conflicting or competing sects based on as many interpretations of the same Bible in the name of same god, same Jesus as the core. What is more each of these sects and denominations boast that their interpretation alone is genuine and all other denominations and religions were abominations of their own denomination. There are simple people to follow each knowingly or stupidly and the leaders get fatter and fatter with the income they derive from their propaganda.

The upshot of all this was the outbreak of violence between religions of different books as well as between different denominations of the same religion based on different interpretations of the same book.

# Chapter 7

# Will Religions Ever Disappear?

In previous chapters we have seen details on various religions and their presence in the world. Now let us embark in evaluate and study whether or not these religions will survive and if yes how long based on our experience with state of religions earlier sprouted and died out, especially on the face of increasing popularity of Atheism and the repercussions there to.

*Atheism* is on the rise universally and sooner or later spirituality could become a thing of the past. A growing number of people - millions worldwide, say they believe that life definitely ends at death – there is no life after death – and that there is nothing like any divine plan for humans. It is an outlook that was there earlier too but is gaining momentum universally of late in the advent of knowledge outbreak of greater dimensions. *Atheism* has never been so much popular as of today in some countries especially in Europe. A *Gallup International Study* of more than 50,000 people in 57 countries indicated that religiosity fell from 77% to 68% between 2005 and 2011 and is still dropping faster and wider.

The world's estimated population of adamant non-believers presently is over 13%. The trend could certainly be a harbinger of things to come, probably if continued, religions someday will disappear entirely. China already has about 200 million Atheists.

## The Atheistic conclusion

The Atheistic conclusion is that the arguments and evidences both indicate there are insufficient reasons to believe the existence of any god, and that religious experiences are just personal and subjective. That is something about the human experiences only rather than the nature of reality itself. Therefore, one has no reason to believe that any god exists. A reality check will prove that what we are taught and made to believe in the past are just myths and tales in the wrested interest to popularize certain doctrines of some communities or groups if one goes by history and science. Say, all religious beliefs are prejudiced.

## The curious question of intellect

This question of whether God exists is heating up in the 21$^{st}$ century much more than before because the world population on the go is getting more educated, sophisticated, enlightened, and moreover curious and intellectual. *Pantheism's* claim is that God is the cosmos and the cosmos is God. In fact, religions should help building values in life like love, empathy, respect and harmony instead of continuing to make people believe in the heaven after earthly life by creating stories and misguiding for profits without any valid proof other than apologues.

Is religion important in today's world is a critical and valuable thought, on the face of advanced philosophical, psychological, social and scientific awareness around us. Moreover, we see that religion is misused by folks to propagate their views, extort money and possessions from ordinary faith-craze population diversifying the weak minds in their ways and live in magnanimous houses with every luxury possible assuring the poor believers of a miraculous heaven after their life in this world. This almost every religion does. There are so many instances the public is fooled to surrender everything they have to the celebrant and live a deficient life to become eligible for heaven. There are a lot of fools to go by that call.

This inhuman tendency is aimed to grasp powers in political world also in much larger scales, we notice in the societies among us. But today a great portion of people began to identify wolfs in sheep's disguise. In practical world most religious leaders act as agents of socialization and extort followers as much as they can. Such individuals and organizations devise their own strategies and methods to execute as we noticed earlier. We can clearly observe that the leaders in most religions are propagating less of scientific and technological awareness, and their own perspective of the scriptures itself is inadequate. One may wonder whether a lot of today's religious leaders focuses on mutual harmony and co-existence or are they really involved in creating disharmony and strife for their own short-term gains. The later seems happening.

**Importance of Religions**

In a way, religions are important as long as they help to shape people's morals, culture, customs, tradition, beliefs and behavior. The birth of religions in the past probably helped humanity to achieve those advantages, but it is not so much today as they deviate into wrong practices. Religious beliefs bound people together like one herd in the past, but today there are distractions of many sorts within believers and the symptoms are on the increase. Moreover, hardcore religious spirituality turned away into creating and corroborating extremism and terrorisms around the globe pitching one group against another in the name of the same '*One God*'!

## Religion and Spirituality

'Religion' and 'spirituality' are two different entities. To prove this, we have to understand the *genesis of religion*. One could doubt if any of the existing religions, in its current form, will help to take us up anywhere higher into a spiritual world. Humans can truly live without religion as we see in our world today, but for many, they cannot live without spirituality. Religion and Spirituality are different, yet they get intertwined due to the lack of consciousness among the people and become tools for conflicts. Some religious skeptics basically believe that you can have religion without God if you have the conviction that something powerful exists beyond the datum of the universe.

It is true that religions have been and still do provide, rarely though, social cohesions to help maintain social solidarity through shared rituals and beliefs; thus, enabling social mechanism to enforce religion-based ethics and norms to help maintain conformity and control in society.

Some believe that religions help to define profound lives of individuals, thus giving meaning to their life and existence itself. At times religious belief in a god they depend helps individuals to deal with the most stressful moment of their lives because it provides hope to overcome present obstacles and move on, whichever god that be. This avoids many from going into depression, so that their life moves in a smooth and healthy manner, which is a sure positive side of religions and one being religious.

## Final Analysis

Therefore, we may say that religious adherence and practices promote the well-being of individuals, families, and communities. Religious worships and gatherings also lead to reductions in the incidents of domestic abuse, crimes, substance abuse, and addiction to drugs and liquor and similar provocative habits. In all, these things contribute to increase in physical and mental overall health, longevity and educational attainments. Religious adherences are promoted in all democratic nations including that of ours even though some people interpret it as the right to fight and wrongly involve in it.

In the conclusive analysis, we find that, with or without religion, good people may do bad things and bad people may do good things or even worse things. It is not essential that all religious people will do only good things and all those without respect to any religion or God will do only bad things. The evidence is before us in our day-to-day life itself. Ever since the cave man began worshipping God and being spiritual, there had been in existence, corrupt activities, crimes, hatred and much more cruel deeds among humans. Sadly, this continues till date.

## The global God divide

What is the connection between belief in God and morality? How important are God and prayers in people's life?

In a research attempt on these questions to 38,000 plus people across 34 countries, spanning six continents, it was found that about 45% said it was necessary to believe in God to lead an ethical life and to possess good values in life. There were large regional variations in answers to these questions but most people had a positive outlook for being religious.

Some people, having realized that no one will ever find true happiness and perfect prosperity without God seek to find him in spiritual ways according to their specific faculties. This is one reason that we have generated many different religions and ideas of God through generations.

The origins of most religions are a matter of debate. Practically all religions have their beginnings from what are called oral traditions. During most of human history, more than 99% of all human beings have been illiterates, having either no education or ability to read or write. Humans throughout did have some sort of language or other means to communicate. Whatever religion they assimilated was gotten through traditions. Most traditions convoluted stories, tales and anecdotes about their various gods, goddesses and sometimes animal deities too.

The most prominent question is *"if God is one, why so many religions to reach that one God?"* It is an assumption, but religions like Hindus would reject the idea that there is just one God. Some religions believe that God simultaneously created *Satan* to mislead people and split their religious realms and split one another in person. It is a marvel that humans devised several paths of their own to reach God. For example, Buddhists don't rely on *'One God'*, their universal *Buddha* has emerged in diverse teachings during diverse times.

Diversity in world religions seems similar. Each religion emphasizes in slightly different aspect of the path toward the holy one. Today it is possible to choose the religion of one's choice, nearest to one's heart, the one that best fits him or her. Although it is a universal practice, some religions strictly prohibit the idea of conversion, and consider such freedom as punishable.

## Hardcore Religious Fanaticisms

Hardcore attitude towards religious beliefs or practices involves uncritical zeal or reflective enthusiasm. Some people display very strict standard and little tolerance for contrary ideas or opinions. Religious fanaticism is devotion to a religion, a form of human fanaticism, which could otherwise be expressed in one's other involvements and participation in dangerous proportion. It is addiction of highest standard in religious activities and beliefs. It is an obsession. Such people may exhibit withdrawal symptoms when they cannot engage in religious activities of their choice. They always feel; it is not enough to be just religious and aim to be totally obsessed. These people actually jeopardize their relationships with other members of the groups as well as other religions. They will have hyper focus on the future and causes to ignore the present and harmony with others in life. Religious fanaticism often results in communal riots and more often in its escalations leading to killings and torture. Any fanatic, especially religious fanatics are very dangerous to peace loving citizens and push back human progress to square one. It is a trend to be controlled by loyal citizens and concerned authorities.

Extremism and terrorism caused by blind fanaticism is a curse of the modern world. It is not important which religion has more fanatics in it but the question is why people turn to fanaticism. Whenever X or Y religion allows fanatics, it is harmful for the entire world.

A 7th century Greek Philosopher from Greece by name Epicurus (341-270 BC) had questioned the existence of God and commented that some people are just fed on the *opium of religious superstition*s from tender age, and conditioned to believe God; but in fact, did not understand what is being taught and what or who is God, and now such people are addicted to this opium and cannot free themselves from such conviction shackles.

A person becomes faithful to a religion when he no longer has any way to realize the reality. When one continues to live that way unquestioned, he becomes a blind follower. When his thoughts reach the state that every other person is against him, he becomes a staunch terrorist who wish to eradicate those who are not on his line of thoughts. In short, all terrorists start with an ordinary mood to follow a religion in which he has no proper knowledge or understanding. At the pinnacle of his behavior pattern, he may become a staunch terrorist wanting to destroy everybody and everything he thinks are against him.

Lastly, there is a group of believers, not necessary in any particular religion, but in most, thinking that their existence is all about God, and that others should respect him or her because of being a great soul in society and wish others should bow before him or her because of his or her such so called position in the society. These people are indeed worthless anywhere else in normal life. They are also not any less than hardcore radicals.

*To be or not to be religious*

# Epilogue

We live in a well-informed society fast advancing with the backup of science and technology in the leading end. Only an educated society can flourish and look forward to grow in the modern age with incredible opportunities ahead of us. Fortunately, we live also in an ideological condition within a secular state having modern outlook and our constitutional supports encourage us to go forward fearlessly in our personal and social lives with full thrust. However, there are two dominant factors, political and religious notions, which are trying to pull us back and ruin our progress to perfection. Some groups seem adamant in executing this attitude in the name of religion.

In spite of our living in the progressive world sustained by good education and all-round developments in all fields, compared to that of yester years, or earlier generations, still we face difficulties in life due to the over encumbrance of religious burdens as evident among us. Our peaceful life is troubled by several religious outrages instead of our expectations of religions supporting morally and enthusiastically. We are drawn back when we surge to go ahead, by religious restrictions and mostly by religious fanatics, whom we fear for disharmony in society and at times even for our life itself. It does not appear the life ahead is any smooth road as long as religions jeopardize and control our social issues and many other attributes in the names of political parties or otherwise.

From the lessons we went through in previous pages of this book, we got to understand the evolution of man's progress in belief in various religions and Gods. Whether mankind would continue to hold religions and gods as central determinant of the future remains to be seen. Some religious groups today lack the right directives and are only created for the existence of few individuals in their best forms swindling its followers. Established religions also have their own differences within their groups and no one knows which one is pure and unselfish. We have also seen that these religions are developed in different countries under different circumstances to meet different purposes of those times. It is difficult to comprehend that they all worship different Gods by naming them differently and preaching different suppositions as situation warrants. Now we are all the more confused as to which is the right one, all of them or none.

Adding to this confusion on deciding a suitable faith group is the establishment of fake media and paid media and the arrival of propaganda wings in many religions, especially in the stronger ones that develop and promote content on social media and other channels that try to paint their perspective as correct and others as wrong thereby all the more confusing perplexed individuals, and also creating an air of disharmony and hatred among them, through their commercial and selfish attitudes.

Several civilizations and faiths all vanished in human history without traces before us. Hundreds of wars were fought in the past in the names of religions and millions of people lost their lives in addition to the destruction it created, we learn from history. We are not sure about the future. One thing is proved that without the help of any religion man can survive and attain progress and that is what we learn from modern society changing to Atheism more and more mainly in developed countries. Only poor and still developing countries in general are holding on to religions as their back bone and that also appears to be heading towards declining in the near future. Valid knowledge can only come from science. Religious beliefs are the remains of pre-scientific explanations of the old world and amount to nothing more than superstitions and speculations. According to vivid arguments if religious institutions are stopped in one generation just like that, then there will be no religions and we will have a more peaceful and more prosperous world to live in without infights and hatred in humanity. Will that happen anytime in the near future is certainly skeptical at this stage.

Whatever, it is apparent that the new generation worldwide is slowly drifting away from religious adherence, practices and rituals and leading a more neutral life and if this trend continues, the future of religions may be in jeopardy.

**Conclusive Observations**

One could wonder, if there is a Universal God, and that God is expected to prevent evil and miseries in the world and save the entire mankind and everything in it; any person with the right mind would think. But as a matter of fact, evil and miseries are part of our lives. Millions are suffering, millions are perishing. The questions then are why we call such a God omnipotent? Or, is the God able to stop evils but not willing; then He is unkind; if God is both able and willing, then why evil prevail? If God is neither able to curtail evil nor willing to do so, why call Him God and surrender before such a deity than believe in oneself and live a liberated and graceful free life?

Having considered most available data relating to religions and faiths, covering human progress from prehistoric times to modern generations, it is the conclusion of the author, that religion and faith are only personal free choices of every individual on earth, and as mandated in modern times by International Human Rights and as accorded by the Constitution of India as well as Constitutions of many countries. The choice of following any particular religion or faith, or no religion at all shall remain a personal choice without pressure from any corner and shall be strictly followed by all people for the benefit of whole mankind, and it shall not be spearheaded to create social disorder and discordances in the world. Being spiritual on the other hand may be an entirely different choice. We have seen that one need not be religious to be truly spiritual. Whether the future generations will choose to be religious, or spiritual, or both, remains to be seen.

Taking a moment to introspect on the following questions that appeared in the social media recently should provide us a meaningful perspective.

Do you demand the doctor who treats you should be of your own religion? No, never, whoever is the doctor I only have to get relieved of my disease;

Do you ask the religion of the person who gives you food when you are hungry? No, what I need is my hunger should subside;

Are you concerned with the religion of your teacher, providing education to you? No, let him be of any religion, all I need is input of educational topics;

Do you ask the religion of person who gives you water when you are thirsty? No, it is only that my thirst must subside and I will say thanks for that;

Do you think religion is important in buying and selling? No, what is needed is money for the seller and commodity for the buyer;

Will anyone ask the religion of the blood donor when you are in dire need for it? No, escaping from death alone is important at such times, whichever the donor is, whatever his/her religion is;

When you hear fun, do you laugh only after checking that it was told by your own religious guy? No, whoever says fun, it is natural for anyone to laugh and enjoy it;

Does pain have religion? No, whoever gets pain will cry from that pain;

Does ability come in persons according to religion? No, it is not a religious choice;

Do you have religion for games? No, Success is everyone's aim;

Is there any fixed time for birth and death? No, when it is time, both will happen;

All the above questions are what we face in our day-to-day life in our present times. Nowhere as above we had our religious guises necessary. In that case where do you exactly need religious concealments? We don't know the answers. But see, neither the rain nor the stream has religion. Sun or moon does not have religion. The earth or sky has no religion. Day or night has no religion. Sea or wind has no religion. Animals and plants have no religion. Then, who has religious complexes? It is only for humans who claim and is proud to have knowledge and social values abundantly but not in reality. Does it look worthy in a world to be divided in the name of religion where all the rest of elements associate with humans in everyday life is common all the same?

It is therefore the contention of the author that no one should force the ideology of his or her religion on another person without his or her will and earnestness, and we should just follow the universal principle of "Live and let live" policy so that we enjoy a pure life of brotherly hood for an harmonious life so long we live as social beings on this earth. Refrain from hate and hard core attitudes to your brothers and sisters following any other religious ideology of their choice because of the fact that they may need religious nourishment to carry on their peaceful and purposeful life, and nothing more. The scope of sustenance of religions in the future is quite contemplatable in the present day settings when appropriated and studied in the ongoing world scenario today.

Let us learn to live peacefully rather than fight in the name of religions. Bygone religious history teaches us only hard times like rivalry, battles, hatred, and loss of life in millions, and not anything good it did. Destiny of man is never spelt authentically by religions. Promises of heaven or afterlife pleasures are not proved fluidities. It is then personal choice for you and me to practice a religion or not especially treating others as rivals and indulging in provocative and harmful methods of any kind.

Having studied so much about from our humble evolution and creation of many religions, and thereby God, their visible affirmative and negative impacts in humanity, it is now for my cherished readers to choose and to decide *"To be or not to be Religious'*.

*"The essence of life is in not being religious on the outside but in being honest and responsible human being, being loved and loving, cared and caring, in good relationship with one another and espousing most compassionate traditions, as well as supporting the humanity to prosper in whichever way one could contribute for fulfillment of that end."*

To contact the author and for more information about his other publications visit:

*www.ChristopherThomas.in*

www.ingramcontent.com/pod-product-compliance
Lightning Source LLC
Chambersburg PA
CBHW031409160726
47993CB00003B/1163